"In her second collection, *Prime*, Jyl Anais has perfected her short lined, spare staccato style. These poems speak with the dead while wading in a deep well of ancestral knowledge. *Prime* is a timely work and worthy follow-up to *Soft Out Spoken*. Consider it a gauntlet thrown by a writer whose poems take no shit."

— Jason Baldinger
A History of Backroads Misplaced: Selected Poems 2010-2020

"when i think of *Prime*, i think of the best meat. in this collection, you get the finest poems. sharp bursts of emotions and imagery. raw, real and human. poems, like 'directions', i find myself standing where she stands, haunted by her poem and my memory. i too once was asked for directions when i was younger. the poem 'sparrow' highlights life and the way the world views people. this or that, black and white. no and goodbye. the ending of this collection softens. brings light. releases everything inside and breathes outward. a torrential collection that grasps but then let's you know all will be okay — life continues."

— John Compton
stranger in the attic of clouds

Prime

jyl anais

Jyl Anais' debut poetry collection, *Soft Out Spoken*, was released in 2019 by Sin Miedo Press. In 2020, she recorded and coproduced *FIRE*, a spoken word album. Jyl's work appears in *Rising Voices: Poems Toward A Social Justice Revolution*, *We Are The Changemakers*, *Santa Clara Review*, *Protectors 2: Heroes*, and *Asylum Magazine for Democratic Psychiatry* among others. Jyl's visual art appears in *Existential Psychology and the Way of the Tao*, *Silent Screams*, and *MONUMENTAL 2021*. Originally from Trinidad, she now lives in the United States. This is her second collection of poetry. Find her at ionc3.com.

Prime

Prime

jyl anais

Sin Miedo Press

First edition
Published by Sin Miedo Press, United States

ISBN: 978-1-387-57861-0

cover & interior design: Jyl Anais

for my ancestors who could not speak their minds for
fear of reprisal & for those who could

They kept trying to

reduce me.

They didn't realize

I was already

a prime number,
indivisible

except
for by myself.

— Prime

This morning
in bed,
I remembered

my black
pussycat boots
with the fake fur
and felt
that I left
when I escaped,

the last time.
And
my green velvet chair.

I left them there.

— There

I am disentangling
myself
from you,

who taught me
that love meant
pain.

— Disentangle

The patriarchy
called.

They said
they want
their power back.

Now, we've gotta fight
like hell just
broke loose.
Because it did.

— The Patriarchy Called
(after Roe vs. Wade was overturned)

I finally understand why
women's anger   is demonized.

In a world that
has been invested
in our   vulnerability,

anger is fundamentally   protective.

— Madness

A white man
in his fifties

pulled up beside me

on my way home
from school

in his nondescript
CIA issued sedan.

I refused
to step closer
to the passenger seat
that separated us.

I knew
he wasn't really
asking me

for directions.

In those moments
we stood
in the afternoon
light,

me, with the weight
of my backpack
heavy along my shoulders,
my eyes
locked

on his,
face fixed
in a stare

that made clear,

"I don't know
what you want.
But you better not fuck
with me.
If you do,
you're gonna
have a fight
on your hands."
The stare he returned

finally surrendered.

Me, with my ancestors
standing
beside me,
just beyond
the veil.
Me, with my spirit towering
over him, fierce and

reflected in my glare.

— Directions

I cannot count
how many times
I have come
close
to that particular danger.

The hair
on the back of my neck stood
gooseflesh shuddered
my nervous system
attuned
to red alert.

I survived them.
Standing beyond arms length
when they stopped
on the side of the road
a girl walking home from school,
while I waited on a bus,
as a woman,

when I went on that date
and never made another.

Now, those who
didn't survive
are my
responsibility.

And because I
can.

— Why?
(for those who ask why I work as a medium with law enforcement)

People
from your ancestral homes

remember you like
they are your distant
cousin, once removed

because
you are.

— Ancestors

your hair
is a poem,
a love letter
from your
ancestors

mailed
from a past
you've
forgotten

— Hair

You can hide
in your apartment,
lock your door,
ignore your friends,
and disconnect.

You can meditate,
go gluten-free,
stop eating refined
sugar, and practice
yoga everyday.

But your karma
will still find you.

Karma will
email you after
not hearing from him
in years.

Karma knows
where you live.
Karma will knock
on your door.
And Karma
won't take no
for an answer.

Karma will call you
on your phone
while you're walking
down the street
even though you
didn't give him your number.

Karma knows

how to talk to you
to get exactly what he
wants, and Karma knows.
Karma knows what he wants.

Do you?

— Karma

Sometimes,
I look
for opportunities
in the wrong places.

That door
I'm knocking on
is really
one to a cage
looking for a bird.

A sales funnel for birds,
if you will.

There's a sign
on the door that says
"Birds Apply Within."
So, I try

and find the door locked.
I knock and knock
and the owner of the cage
looks out his window
and says,

nothing or
"Sorry, you're not the kind
of bird
we're looking for."

And I think,
"But I'm a bird!
Let me in!"

He's looking for
sparrows,

not eagles.

Those cages
weren't built
for the kind of bird
I am,
too small and weak
to hold me.

— Sparrows

The anger

is on slow
burn today

last night it
erupted
in cities and towns
across
America

in my town
in my community
in my heart

tattooed
on monuments,
spray paint
emblazoned
on
the Confederacy

in a culture
still fighting the
Civil War

and we're
on the brink
of it now,
again
here,
with the Nazis
and their
sympathizers
in unmarked
uniforms

with shield
and gun
brandishing
their masculinity
for all the world
to see
who's really in
control.

— The Anger

I am a
West Indian woman.
So, I fit into many
categories,
none of them, neatly.

Except one:
Other.

I am a
West Indian woman,
which is to say
I am of mixed race.
My ethnicity
spans continents
and across seas,
a result of
generations of
Transmigration.

Not white,
not black,
not red
not brown but
all of those.

I came from drums
with voices that floated through
Port of Spain,
on a breath blown along
the surface of the sea
from a town with the same name
as the local mad house.

I'm not "playing white"
or claiming to be

a member of an oppressed
group I don’t belong to.

I came from rape,
too many times to number.
I came from injustice.
I came from tamarind,
soursop, and ripe mango.
I came from rum and jungle
to “What are you?
Chinese?” and
“Why don't you go back
to where you came from?”

with a face from too many places.

I wasn’t welcome
into a gathering of the
Third World Alliance
though I am an immigrant
from the Third World.
Should I show you
my papers?

I came from
fertile ground,
transplanted into earth
saturated with Roundup,
then commanded to
make something of myself:
“Grow!”
they shouted.

Shut up.
Smile.
Accommodate.

Assimilate.

So many expectations to live up to
with skin too light and
a culture too dark to be
fully included anywhere.

With ancestry spread
across nations, bloodlines
drawn across the globe

thin like patience.

— Patience [i]

the cobbler said
my shoes
were too broken
to be fixed

with their soles
worn,
and their material
deteriorated.

and I think
of
the variety
of Stepford wives
that surround me
driving
black Mercedes, who
fly to conferences
on their own dime,

with their debutante balls
and pedigrees.

I just want
my shoes fixed
so I can wear
them, again,
the ones that fit
and ground me,
their soles intact.

— the shoes that fit

To those
without
the knowledge
you possess,

your knowledge
is simply belief.

As Jung said,
"Beware
of unearned
wisdom."

Know
what you
know.

— Warnings

Some soldiers
return home.
They leave the war
even when the war
never leaves
them.

Flags fly
in their honor,
celebrated
as heroes.

And some soldiers
have to
keep fighting
the wars
embedded
in culture.
Battle lines drawn
at home.

With no
safe place,
to return.

No flags fly.
No honor.
No titles.
For bodies who are
their own nations
marked by
violation
after violation.

Death counts.
The wounded walk.

— Death Counts

How many ways
can I say
"I'm not dating
your resume?"

You can put your dick
back in your pants,
take your SEAL training
and your surgical skills,
get in your Jaguar,
and take the next exit back onto
the superhighway
of samsara.

Because I'm not
auditioning to be your
next trophy wife,
and I'm not
your mistress,
a woman you can call
when you're bored
with your wife or
when it's convenient,
in between your
real
priorities.

If your wife can't trust you,
neither can I.

I may have wandered into
the arctic wilderness of your heart,
but I'm an emotional survivalist
and can find my own way home.

I'm not an accessory

or a toy to play with.
My dignity
will always be worth
more to me
than unlimited access
to your assets.

I could be a spiritual master,
incarnation of a goddess,
accomplished artist,
attend a college more difficult
to get into than Harvard,
have a heart of gold,
model on the latest runway,
use remote viewing
to help solve a sexual homicide,
speak to the dead regularly,
be as loyal
as the sun
rising every morning,
but in your eyes
I'll always be reduced
to my tits and ass.

You do know how to divide by
the lowest common denominator.
I know I'm only as valuable
as how often
you want to fuck me.

I don't give a shit
about your PhD,
your BMW,
or that you won
the biggest verdict
in history.

What I care about
is the way you treat me.

— The Superhighway of Samsara [ii]

I look
down
for inspiration,

as most light
that comes from above
is reflected,

but light
is everywhere.
All matter is
light and space,

fields of consciousness
vibrating.

— Light

I can
feel
your
heart
heavy
today

like
it
beats
in
my own
chest.

— My Own

I found
a love letter,
today,

that I wrote
20 years ago
to my
future self.

It said,
"You're like
a sparkler
that never
goes out."

— Sparkler [iii]

Tonight,

the sky was
a desert.

But my spirit
was bright enough
to find
my own way
home.

— Tonight

the world
is on fire,
but we're
still falling
in love

and that
makes
the heat
more
tolerable

— on fire

Your
words
will
be
a key.

Speaking
them
will
unlock
the
cage,

even
if
it is
quietly
to the sky.

— The Key [iv]

The End

Notes

---

[i] "Patience" was originally published in *Santa Clara Review, Volume 109, Issue 1.*

[ii] "The Superhighway of Samsara" was originally published in *Horror Sleaze Trash*, 2021.

[iii] "Sparkler" was originally published in *Ethel 10, Fall 2022.*

[iv] "Key" was originally published in *Ethel 10, Fall 2022.*

We offer discounts if you would like to order 10 or more copies of *Prime*. Email us through the contact page at ionc3.com for our discount schedule. Thank you.

www.ingramcontent.com/pod-product-compliance
Ingram Content Group UK Ltd.
Pitfield, Milton Keynes, MK11 3LW, UK
UKHW041644190726
13854UKWH00006B/2684

9 781387 578610